This page is intentionaly left blank.

© 2019 Charles T. Thompson

Charles T. Thompson
Poems of Persuasion: One Knee or Two? Are You Praying Or Are You Begging?

All rights reserved. No part of this publication may be reproduced, stored in a retrieval system or transmitted in any form or by any means, electronic, mechanical, photocopying, recording or otherwise without the prior permission of the publisher or in accordance with the provisions of the Copyright, Designs and Patents Act 1988 or under the terms of any license permitting limited copying issued by the Copyright Licensing Agency.

Published by: HRM Incorporated — Publishing Div.

Editor: A.C. Bryan

Illustrations By: J Marcus

Cover Design by: Geana Harris

Artwork By: Justus Maxwell Thompson

ISBN-13: 978-0-9908788-8-9

Charles T. Thompson

Poems of Persuasion: One Knee or Two?
Are You Praying Or Are You Begging?

HRM Incorporated

Poems of Persuasion: One Knee or Two?

Are You Praying Or Are You Begging?

CHARLES T. THOMPSON

Contents

Note From The Author	13
You Will Still Be My Mother	17
No Poetic Words Needed	18
You Must Be My Better Half	21
Blind Trust	24
Never	25
Rebound	26
Patience and Persistence	28
Personal Growth Is Not Physical	29
Is Your Man Above Average?	30
I Guess A Woman Wants...	32
The World For My Lady	33
No Title Required	34
Jasmine... A Flower	35
I Don't Want A Poem	36
Spectrum of Color	38
Light and Life	39
Light On This Side	40
A Zebra's Stripes	41
Colorado	42
A Lemon Drop Shot?	43
Quiet Desire	44
Need, Wants, & Desire	45

Rain...	46
Wind...	47
Wet Spot?	48
Wandering Lust	49
Jealousy	50
Passion In The Face of Rejection	51
Betrayal Is A Conscious Trial	52
When...	53
Decisive	54
... Is Like...	55
Both Sides of the Napkin	56
From Here To There	58
To Paris And Back...	59
Why Do I Need Thee?	60
Romance Lost	61
Parenting Alone	62
When I'm Done, I'm Done	63
Secrets...	64
I Will Lie	65
Unfaithful	66
Frustration	67
Loss	68
Enigma	69
Trust Beyond Compare	70
Attention	71
Intent	72

A Whisper... Don't You Know?	73
The Smile I Asked For...	74
Innocence Behind A Smile	75
The Joy In The Smile That I Gave You	76
Who Is Concerned About My Lips?	77
What Do I Have to Apologize For?	78
Unappreciated Beauty	79
I Do See...	80
Bees	81
Want and Won't	82
Poetic Words	83
Me, We, Us	84
You & Me, Became Us	85
Mirror 4U or Us	86
Your Birthday	87
Courage	88
Being In Love...	89
Ambition	90
To Be Honest	91
Can't... Now What?	92
Moved- Inside Out?	93
Missed Connections	94

Future, My Happiness & Acceptance	95
A Final Chat	96
Thought	99
Awareness	100
Loyalty?	101
A Greater Loyalty	102
Sense It, Feel It, Trust It	103
Consistency	104
Infinity	105
Testing The Principle of Discretion	106
Nothing	107
Look Up	108
Presence	109
Searching	110
Hope?	111
Insecurity and Beauty	112
I'm In A Dark Room	114
Integrity With Personal Amendments	116
The Danger of Logic	117
Consume Ideals...Digest Reality	118
Will, Fate & Grace	119

What's The Difference?	120
Translucent, Opaque, and Transparent	121
Are We Truly Grateful?	122
Breathe and Let Go	123
Why Are We Here?	124
Treasure, Recognition and Purity	125
So, What Is Earthly Success?	126
Things More Important Than $...	127
Humble	128
Earthly to Spiritual?	129
Vision For A Blessing	130
This Side of Calm	131
Why Can't You Stay?	132
Find Me...	134
Heavenly Father, When I	135

Note From The Author

Poems of Persuasion is a lifelong, collection of thoughts captured on napkins and scraps of paper. These collections, which may have been inspired by events— not all true— or invoked by a simple request in order to explain circumstances... These thoughts are shared in this medium; as a means by which to shed light or provide insight.

Not every collection is for everyone, nor will all these so-called poems have an instant connection to every consumer. However, I believe there must be at least one poem that will resonate with each reader. Please note, there are no dates or time references surrounding each poem, as time and dates are not relevant to interpretation. Regardless, I trust the poems will be enjoyable.

There may be more collections in the future— if the pen has ink, the thoughts and circumstances still continue to flow, and, of course, with a constant supply of napkins.

A favor before you start to consume the words. There are some recurring themes that I feel obligated to share: God's Grace is one; to be blessed, is truly humbling. The concept of a smile— the act, given or received, will change your day.

Beauty is explained, expressed, or referenced at least 43 times in this work. Your actions, reactions, and interpretation of beauty will be innate to you; be open and kind in what beauty causes your senses to reveal.

It is my sincere hope that all your senses will be touched at some point. That said, it is not recommended to attempt to read all these words in one sitting. Like great cake and ice cream, take it in slices and scoops.

Please allow me to first thank God for the patience required to capture, then convert all the napkins and scraps of paper into this collection. I want to thank my family and friends for their unwavering love and support as they helped to remove self-doubt and self-pity during the creation, collection, and editing. For that and in all things, I am truly grateful!

You Will Still Be My Mother

When I grew up and moved away,
Visited home and did not stay;
Went out in the morning and returned at dawn,
Since the day I was born— You were my Mother.

If I cried out and lost all shame,
Found new religion and changed my name,
Lost my job and self-esteem
Forgot all my hopes and life-long dreams...
You would still be my Mother.

Centuries from now, when we have long left this earth—
No dollar signs, credits cards, or even net worth;
When God has taught us all to love each other...

You will still be my Mother!

No Poetic Words Needed

When it comes to family,

                      no poetic phrases are required;

yet the desired intent
is time well spent,

                better still valuable moments remembered.

We have journeyed and enjoyed Phoenix to Houston,
and no less than a complete unit filled with bliss.
With each moment and every kiss we grow;
with each passing birthday, holiday, and major milestone,
we know, no poetic phrases are more important than,

                        "I Love You!"

Yes, because we are family, and Love is part of our soul!

You Must Be My Better Half

You are truly my better half...
To sustain such a positive attitude with all the negative energy around you...

both personal and professional.

Please continue to remain positive,
because my only joy right now
is knowing that you are happy.

The most self-less thing I can ever do,
as your husband,
is to ensure your happiness,
regardless of
how I feel.

It would violate my personal constitution to pretend
that I am happy with certain circumstances,
when I am not.
With that, I must apologize that the realities of life have beaten
me down to this state.

Realities being what they are,
I will not and cannot ignore them.

Pray for me.

What Are You Hiding In There?

What are you hiding in there?

The view from the outside is pleasant...
but it's not the present, WE believe you hide.

It is the vision, that remains constant, in the viewer's mind's eye.

> We feel your pulse, with each and every smile, dimples displayed...

a glance too soft to touch, that reflects your hearts true beat;
But it is the purity in your soul, that makes US rise to our feet.
Still, you are hiding something in there, that our earthly vision cannot grasp or comprehend.

So, we must stop there before our earthly minds and thoughts condemn, the luxury of GOD's creation, painted on life's canvas to remove strife.

Because what is not hidden in there, is how you bless and honor everyone with grace;
enabling an extraordinary experience called true life!!

Why Are We Here?

There is an undeniable,

    undisputed

        truth of why

           we

                are

                    here.

Yet, as we search for the excuses to explain our absence and relapses into lost time, we realize that unfiltered joy IS not at the top of our list.
    Dare we suggest that lost time ensures we are conscious of joy, filled with passion...
        perceived and therefore realized by the emotion with the notion of accountable time?
        Simply put, we lose time...
For the pure joy that we have IT to use, however, when it cost us more, why do we lose our way?

Why are we here? We are trying to recapture lost time and valuable ways to fill it.

Blind Trust

Let's discuss, if we must...

                    blind trust.

When we drive, do we fear being alive?
Trusting those who give permits and licenses,
to those who are on the road?

Do we care if the origin of our food is here or there;
Or what nutrients our food consumed,
could change how our sustenance is prepared?

Is the blind trust we graciously give to those who cross our path and unknowingly impact it...
Are they worthy of knowing that they did?

It would not matter as much, if all things went as planned;
        no detours, no disasters, no detrimental acts...
                imagine this, if you can?

If everyone considered all human beings around them and treated them as such,

                    blind trust would be irrelevant;
the innate gift of kindness would shift from self, and the joy of interaction would be worth twice as much!

Never

Never looked at you...

                                                but I should have;

Never looked past your smile...

                                                but I could have.

Never accepted the crown...

                                                but I might have,

              simply because it was yours.

Never wanted all that you had to offer,

                                        but I should have asked,
                              and then asked for more.

Never, should have said never;

    It does not guarantee what I desire and wish to see you for...

                        never again.

Rebound

A rebound is much more than a basketball action.

It is the reaction,
when the "balls of life", we juggle daily,
get dropped,
and WE
bounce
back.

Let's define the balls:

Ball #1 — is wooden, represents every day stuff. When you drop it, it does not bounce; yet when its landing is not where you're standing. You can come back and pick it up.

Ball #2 — is glass, represents relationships. If you drop them, it may break or hurt, but you can put the ball back together. Maybe the reflected light will travel thru differently, and the new spectrum will be better.

Ball #3 — is porcelain, representing health and family. No matter how much they irritate us, they are all we have. If we drop it, it cannot be replaced or repaired.

Ball #4 — is rubber and it's YOU! If you drop it and can REBOUND, it will bounce. Don't let the other balls drop, but don't let the rubber one bounce too long.

Patience and Persistence

Patience and persistence are two keys in life,
        and success is only one of the doors they open...
Why do they dissolve in the hands of the average man?

        Do you see me as average?

This poem is dedicated to those who are above average.

Patience requires the ability to wait,
        without words or emotion,
            when all is lost, yet with God's Grace,
our path is re-found.

Persistence mandates the ability to ask, without asking;
to know without being arrogant, and to command all without
being annoying.

Then there is the concept of utopian thought...

Pause for the silence contained inside deep thought, and all
        that can be shared when asked nicely.

What would you prefer?
        Patience with persistence, or without?
        Regardless, the constant energy is because of you!

Personal Growth Is Not Physical

Personal growth is not physical, if you think so, you miss the point.

To be 'better' than you are now, is why we stretch to see over the next hill.

Can you imagine the 'better' me?

If not, leave me alone!

If so, embrace the fact that when we are 'better,'

WE WILL BE BETTER!

And then, the physical growth, naturally comes.

All that said, never underestimate the ebb and flow of life....
each valley provides a hill to climb, and with each step,

I WILL, and CAN BE BETTER.

Is Your Man Above Average?

An above average man has an acute appetite for someone who has natural beauty, intelligence, and sexual presence...

Is this the essence of you?

An above average man must be fed, not just in bed, but his mind and ego too.

Do you have the ability to be self-less and selfish as the moment requires?

To yield, push back, sustain; or truly submit to his desires? When he loses his way and his sanity nearly escapes him, will you guide him with tough love?

An above average man, generally does not lack confidence, motivation or even a moral compass...

Yet are these the best characteristics that describe him?

Can his silence be enough, when you feel words must be shared? Will you listen even though no words are being said?

Will you forgive the few moments, when he approaches being average with as much enthusiasm when he hovers above all?

An above average man will not deceive you about who he is, who he was and where he wants to go....

Because if your man is not above average, could that be a direct reflection on you?

Or to repeat, is that simply the essence of you?

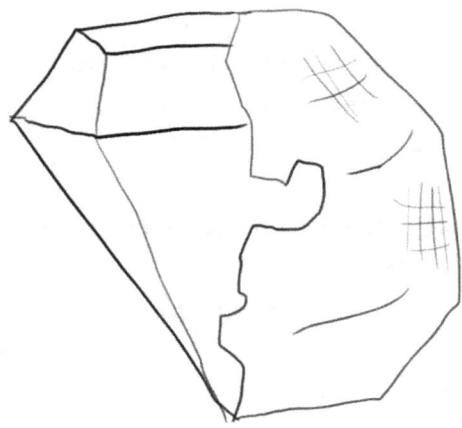

I Guess A Woman Wants...

What a woman wants from a man, starts with what she IS NOT willing to accept.

I would guess a woman,

        not a girl,

does not WANT a boy,

        but a man,

to look past her for another,
even if she is approached by a brother,
less respected and viewed more often by some.

I would bet that she does not NEED a man with money,
but HAS CHARACTER,
who can appreciate the conversation after,
the mood and moments before;
just because he is and may be the only man,
she ever saw with both the attributes all in one.
I am sure, that she can endure, love lost,
because lust is never enough,
that trust is earned,
and loyalty is mutual with the guiding principle that a LADY,
can be 'THAT B****',

        that MOTHER

                and THE WOMAN...

that's it AND I'm done!

The World For My Lady

Frustration starts when my Lady does not have all she needs. The frustration gets extended when she can't have what she wants or desires.

Can you imagine the frustration when I think I fail as a man,
                    a husband and a father,
just because I don't anticipate the problems in front of us?

So when I believe I am on top of my game,
have no shame in my actions,
something surfaces to cause an innate and internal pain.
My Lady, My Wife,
the mother of my last child and the love of my life;
deserves and will have all that I am and all that I will be,
regardless of my own frustration.

The life she makes for US, is greater than I ever imagined...
                  for that I am grateful.

The world she is preparing for our son, will eclipse anything that I could ever imagine.

            For this, I will continue to give my Lady,
            the world,
            with all that I have and all that I don't.

No Title Required

U R a strong woman and a stronger mother.

Our children pass thru our lives,

                              they don't define it.

All we can do is teach and love them with GOD's Grace...

                You have done that very well!!

Jasmine... A Flower

A flower by another name.

Oops,
written and said already, wouldn't want to steal or sound the same;

Can a world of historic views and triumphant thoughts encompass the beauty of this flower...
Jazmin?

All senses are elevated when THIS flower is present or presented;
One should feel conflict when smell wants to take over for sight and when sight might yield to touch.

As such, the feel and sexual appeal must be given with complete reverence and respect,

As this special flower, untouched, unseen and untasted, IS wasted on way too many!

I Don't Want A Poem

I don't want a poem, I want to be with you.
You should know that words, alone, don't impress me.
I don't want to like you, because, I want to be with you AND
like is not enough for me.

Try this:

Every moment, every ounce of energy,
every piece of food sustains life....

Give me THAT and nothing less..
Give me the BEST and make those words you speak so well
true;
Do these things and I am with you!!

OR

A poem without a title, no inspiration required,
just your presence....
STOP!

To figure out what something IS, you must first, figure out what it IS NOT.

Clouds, stars, sunshine and rain;
Hopelessness, mediocracy and pain.

Where does the joy come from?
Within the soul of those who consume the love given from a distance?

Can you see ME, seeing YOU and never having to write, share or enjoy a poem written for YOU with NO TITLE?

Spectrum of Color

Recently, I was looking for a color-filled rainbow;
one with multiple colors appeared...
colors too close to separate.

>Historically, my expectations have been so focused
>on a concise and finite spectrum of color;
>that the brilliance of the reflected light was missed.

So, my future thoughts will guarantee light and color intersect, so that my vision of the expanded spectrum could only be stopped by a total eclipse;

>AND yet,

>thru all this,

the illumination of your beauty will never be impacted.

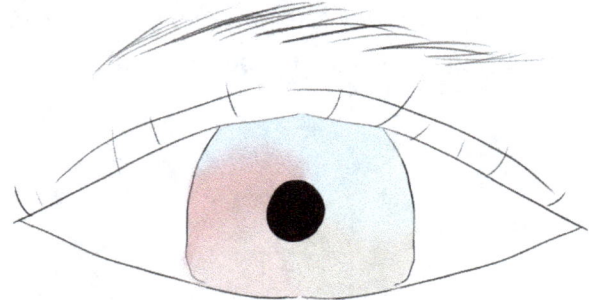

Light and Life

LIGHT and LIFE intersect, in beauty and in darkness.

Not everyone can harness the energy emitted by natural causes.
Can you imagine the sustained momentum the inverse view of internal trust would cause?

It would encourage us to view ourselves in a LIGHT,
that might force inter and introspection

OR

cause us to find the reflection beyond the image given to us by others.

The moments we LIVE,
are not and cannot be overshadowed by how LIGHT,
nor the weight of LIFE we enjoy.

Light On This Side

The light on THIS SIDE,
is only bright when you smile;

>STOP:

>>Who are we lying to?
>>There is a light just because you are around.

Intelligence forces us to ask why we DON'T do what we should, would, or could;

>because
>we
>can't.

We recant, or forgive, the things that remove light from OUR existence;

>>and yet,
>>the resistance that those who feel they are special,
>>always mandates that we do more;

More for those who see US in the light and the dark.
Those who NEED us regardless of our losses.
Those who WANT us because of who we simply are.
>Full of imperfections, insecurities, and doubt...
>Yet through it all,
>YOU are the LIGHT,

and one thing I can ill afford to live my LIFE without, on THIS
>SIDE.

A Zebra's Stripes

Imagine the stripes on a zebra,
not being the division of black and white;

Continue to imagine, that the purpose of a zebra's tail is not to swat a fly that causes disruption,

        but to PROTECT an integrated WORLD;

Continue to imagine, the beauty of the stripes blended;
Because a zebra is not a horse, donkey, or mule;
    yet a mix of those things that make THIS WORLD REAL!

Colorado

More than a state,
    more than a destination,
        more like an institution,
            yet truly an attitude.

        Such is the difference between a dancer,
            a stripper,
    or maybe you don't know.

As if someone would prefer to engage in discussion
    with no direction
    or destination in site,
    and still try to grow?

        Better still, why is honesty so easy,
        yet the absolute truth is so painful?

Never look past those who look upon you,
when you look upon them with trust and without the innate
    expectation of your joy!
    Representation of THIS WORLD.

A Lemon Drop Shot?

Let's start with the ingredients:
Triple sec with lemon —

>   just tart enough, but necessary

as is your smile when completely consumed;

>   vodka,
>
>   alcohol, that cures all,
>
>   as your presence does for most and sugar,
>
>   the sweetest of all nature's joy, as is the taste of your...

>   Pause.

A lemon drop shot is how you shoot in and out of my space,
a place I would like you more often....

>   Bottoms up!!

Quiet Desire

To close one's eyes and still see
the vision that makes your soul smile;

To move beyond the physical
to imagine utopian bliss takes a while.

It is the quiet desire that drives one to be content with silence
and the gracious sound it emits.

Commit to this desire and the silent sound is truly

eu

phor

ic.

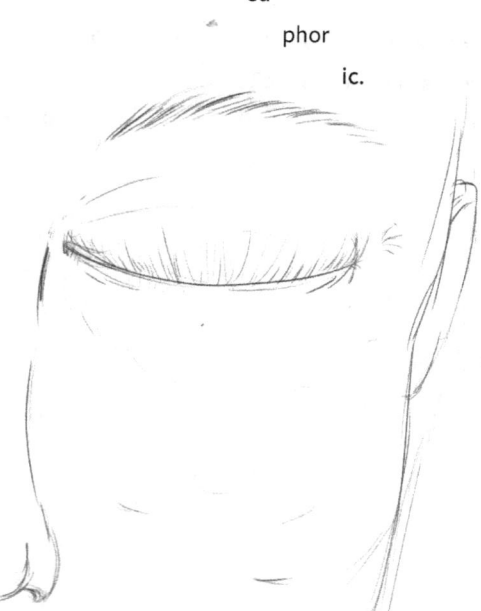

Need, Wants, & Desire

I wasn't hungry,

        but the food I NEED is in your soul;

I wasn't thirsty,

        but the fluids a visionary WANTS

        will come from your eyes,

                or so I am told.

I wasn't sleep,
yet the rest I DESIRE,
has to happen externally

        in

          your

            arms.

        So if your DESIRE,
        your WANTS,
        and what you NEED
        are met by me...

        Eat slowly with my soul in mind,
        drink with the vision you see through my eyes,
        and rest with the notion true love can never,
        ever cause any harm!

Rain...

The constant rhythm of rain spurs the desire
we to share LOVE between those who want a MOMENT.
    These raindrops that prepare us to share a MOMENT
        don't always excite our soul;
Just like the beauty we drink in often misses its role...
water, the result of rain, extends life.
    It is the randomness in the pattern, the beat,
        which we hear in the raindrops;
that causes the intensity we require,
that documented time cannot alter.
    Find rain's rhythm that allows the mutual energy,
        enthusiasm and desire that yields a MOMENT.

Wind...

Listen to the WIND,
sharing the words of nature;
Speaking to US,

>> yet I
>>
>>   can't
>>
>>   reach
>>
>>   you.

Listen to wisdom that someone shared,
yet you did not hear them for stubbornness.
The quality of company escapes YOU —
not because you CAN'T have someone,
you choose NOT TO…

>> You can't call it loneliness,
>> because BY CHOICE,
>> you choose to be alone.

> Loneliness in YOUR case is for the lack of desire to share,
> to risk all.

What is given by some, taken for granted by too many…
innate to a few, the CHARACTER that exists in me,
is similar to how the wind can shape what I actually have to offer YOU…

> So listen to the WIND!

Wet Spot?

A few thoughts on an average Monday—
        a slow day,

                              when it rained,
the sun shined and still a wet spot was easy to find;
then we left the weather behind,
captured our real thoughts, to seek JOY...

Wait, wait, joy has no parameters,
no questions and truly no reason,
just as rain and euphoric joy have no season.

What words and expressions can we share and enjoy,
or express for the endless thoughts that cause the 'rain' to be
internal versus external?

    What notion moves us from the old potion to the new?
    What made the wet spot be caused by me and not you?

        Every moment we share is endless,
      when we have something that leads to the wet spot.

Wandering Lust

Wandering lust as explained to me is the desire to travel.

The cave man's mind, interprets this to mean, physical travel; yet the intellectual part of his being is moved to the metaphysical.

What happens at the intersection of heart, mind, body, and soul?

What positive collision results when we allow ourselves to be moved by the mere existence of another?

Is it an accident at all,
when the friction of human contact causes reactions of all kinds at this purpose filled, metaphysical intersection?

Let's just appreciate the fact that we all hope to be moved and want to have wandering lust, both physical and metaphysical.

Enjoy each opportunity, each moment and each movement.

Jealousy

        Jealousy asked me to look that way,
        when I should have looked the right way.
        Jealousy encouraged me to speak a certain way,
        when I should have had nothing at all to say.
        Jealousy forced me to act this way,
        when no acts should have caused me to pay.

Pay?

        Oh...

Pay for the precious moments granted
when compensation wasn't the question;
Pay for GOD's Grace,
when only prayer and obedience are simple suggestions.
Pay for the decisions and consequences
of those less informed than US.

Jealousy makes US find a path thru life,
we PERCEIVE are our own decisions,
YET we will discover, eventually,
that OUR steps, OUR actions, and OUR reactions
are governed by something, someone which is greater.

        So we may yield to jealousy,
        but we MUST kneel to HIM!

Passion In The Face of Rejection

The feeling

(fear)

of rejection

trumps the empty emotion of having
what we DON'T want.

When we have what we DO want,
why do we reject
the natural sense of joy and peace?

Pause for a moment

to contemplate

the concept of extended passion in the face of rejection...

without fear.

Too often the focus is on
'one sided submission'
without mutual and beneficial exchange.
The values, principles, and character of one's soul
pauses the passion and increases the intense fear of rejection.

Try this:

we are here, this is the moment....

reject rejection, and embrace passion in its purest form -

pleasure.

Betrayal Is A Conscious Trial

Betrayal is a conscious trial, no better than a lie.
The truth is based on facts,
yet the absolute truth is based on accountability.

Never have those who wanted more, given less
to be more than they should be based on what they said,
yet had their words be untrue.

Hey, where is the absolute truth in what you said?

Leave it to the naive to believe
that what they desired to be unattainable.
Again, "we are the decisions that we make".
Your betrayal was that you did not choose me and that's the absolute truth!

When...

Find what it takes to trust;
without that, what you like, want, and desire
will not make any sense;
nor will you ever have what you need.

> Discover how the precious resource of time is spent.
> Without that, you will never be able to let go
> of the fact that there is never enough...
> time.

Desire— both mental and physical— are connected.
Say "YES" with blind, unmitigated trust, and all will be yours.

Disappointment is a self-regulated feeling.
With Trust, Created Time, and Unmitigated Desire,
YOU should never be disappointed!

WHEN?

Decisive

> A person's eyes will not change based on gravity.
> The innate forces that move most objects
> cannot move determination.

Depth has no inertia,
meaning has no bounds,
as being decisive has no right or wrong.

> Someone once said,
> TWO wrongs don't make a right,
>
> but THREE lefts do...

Look upon me, as if my presence and the sound of my voice have you in suspended awe...

> unwavering and DECISIVE...

> then decide.

... Is Like...

Capturing one more moment...
or maybe a few
OR simply trying to release a thought or two?
Critical is the criticism that came with 'that' view;
YOU were selected, not assigned and that is absolutely true!

The presence of positive energy,
IS LIKE the natural rhythm in a series of words.
The reception of syncopated synergy,
IS LIKE passing on a parfait, with fruit, that would be absurd!
The acceptance of chemistry, as art & science,
IS LIKE the essence of self-acknowledgement,
something I really prefer.

Both Sides of the Napkin

It is not my poetic preference to write on both sides of the napkin; in this case, I must.

The words are not easily flowing, and for this reason, I ask you to follow and trust.

My mind drifts to the less fortunate, who struggle for hope, when there is none to be found.

Just as I write these words, on the front side of the napkin, when no one is around.

I use the napkin to capture a collection of words, sponsored by circumstances and time spent.

Others use the napkin to hide their true emotions; to wipe away the tears, because of these events.

Some use the napkin to cleanse a space, to wash away the filth, sorrow and dismay.

Some use the napkin to capture shame or to dispose of articles... sadly, the other side of the napkin IS NOT the start of a new day.

It is simply the opportunity to reorganize words, after the first draft, as I attempt to refresh words in an original way.

What if a napkin was not disposable and we had to reuse them….. what would we use them for?

Pardon me, if I stop here, as this collection seems to have hit a dead end….

so, I will flip the napkin over and begin collecting once more.

From Here To There

> From here to there,
> being rubbed right and wrong;
> for words without a song,
> you dance.

Yet, romance doesn't start with the rub,
it starts with the smile;
is extended by the dimples,
and solidified by confidence not lost.

> But what about the intangible cost of chance;
> in which the conversation that leads to the discussion
> in which being rubbed is confirmed
> to be a positive circumstance?

> Be rubbed from here to there...

To Paris And Back...

To Paris and back,
it is a fact that beauty is in the eyes of the beholder,
>at least that is what he told her.

Then he tried to 'wine her and dine her,
so that at the end of the night,
he could be 'behind her;'
>and you know the rest....
>Thx for the thoughts and actions she said,
>>but I WANT a woman.

>Can you help me?

>Paris, should not be embarrassed to express herself;
>If she NEEDS a man and WANTS a woman and HE is a MAN,
>>HE should help her to Paris and back!

Why Do I Need Thee?

Why do we need THEE?

Because WE will never ever look past you,
YOUR joy is quite easy to see.
Unparalleled joy is expressed when WE
look inward for confirmation,
even if we must bend a knee.

GOD has blessed YOU with a child
to bounce on that same, bent knee,
yet is the greater joy still within YOUR reach?
Don't allow external pressures to diminish why
WE ALL need THEE!

Romance Lost

I'm not good at asking the question
OR expressing the emotion.
I think it's hard to convey the message of romance.

Therefore, I don't and can't consider
NOT enjoying this single, simple moment.
Don't pass me by, until we find...

                      ROMANCE LOST!

Parenting Alone

Feel me, parenting alone, yet still not fully grown...
still having to be the mother and father, that society expects or intends;

Society...
intentionally judges and labels me in the wrong percent,
with or without an accent,
because we are not meeting their expectations.
Whose expectations are most important?
The son or daughter I must raise as the baby daddy
or baby momma moves on, I remain, underpaid!

When do I ever get to become the man or woman
I once believed I should be,
before the bundle of joy, graciously given to me,
changed my ability to be less than I wanted?
When will it be safe to share my space,
my complete world with someone worthy.

Are they worthy?

I can't serial date,

as I must provide and protect those who will pass thru my life, but don't define it!

Feel me, as I drop to both knees and ask....
"GOD, Grant me the serenity to accept the things I cannot change;
courage to change the things I can,
and the wisdom to know the difference (Prayer)!"[1]

---

[1] reference to the Serenity Prayer by theologian, Reinhold Niebuhr.

When I'm Done, I'm Done

I did not want some and none was what I would have gotten;
I only wanted to enjoy the idea of being spoiled rotten.
The rottener I was, the more irritated I became
with the stages AND phases
AND events AND lack of intimacy that can't be repeated.

Standing inline...
waiting...
for the person I desired...
never had, and somehow lost?

What?

Did I say I was done?
Maybe the absolute truth is,
I never really got started...
still when I'm done, I'm done!

Secrets...

The other side of a secret can cause an inverse view of the truth;

> The reality is, the secret sauce,
> the secrets to hiding capital gains and loss,
> the secrets to success...
> Are there more than one?

The list has just ended, before the story has begun.
A secret can motivate one,
to be more than they imagined,
Like a black lie is more tragic than the absolute truth.

> Be cautious, when seeking to find secrets,
> as gaps in someone's character;
> If they don't have IT, whatever
> IT IS, they don't know,
> can't grow IT
> and surely can't buy IT.

It has been said, that CHARACTER and TEMPERAMENT change
under my dominance.
Lives ONCE touched by become TUNED...

THERE AIN'T NO SECRET IN THAT!

I Will Lie

I will lie about the joy your mere presence brings;
I will lie about the way I am fed—

>   not because of food, drink, or your bed.

I will lie about being weak,

>   to ask for a text or pic...

>   >   whatever it takes to not be alone.

When I am on the edge of losing it or not finding my way, I will lie to get you to talk me off the ledge.

>   So, what will I NOT lie about?
>   Nothing, if I would lose your respect.

Everything, as long as I have the time to make the lies true, for

>   you!

Feel me?

Unfaithful

Unfaithfully, they acted and explained to me,
not about emotion, but purely physical, said SHE.
How do I tell HIM, with complete honesty,
that he still is the one who has the mystical,
musical, and magical motion to fill the moment?

> A momentary loss of direction,
> without affection,
> but still passion filled?
> Remember the honesty...
> Until the second moment was offered
> and accepted and fulfilled?

Now the crossroads of the absolute truth are in front of us;
The events and moments connected
were full of emotion never experienced,
yet is HER mind stronger than her body?

> Tell HIM, deal with the consequences
> of lust lost and love gained!
> Will he accept HER being UNFATITHFUL?

Frustration

Frustration is that place in your mind,
where time and circumstance have caused patience to escape;
   To be frustrated by the actions of the ignorant,
     is to not use the GOD given intelligence granted you.
              To be frustrated by the arrogant,
                    facilitates their ego
                and their desire to embarrass you
                    into not using your mind.
To be frustrated by the ridiculous is absurd;
they would be better served,
       if you never uttered a word.

   To be sure, frustration lives and must be managed by you
AND should not be directed at those who cannot and do not know.

To excuse the ignorant,
      the arrogant,
           and the ridiculous,
                  releases frustration in the right way.

Loss

As we dance to the songs of life
our self-imposed expectations grow.
Did you know that embracing negativity causes loss?
Loss, defined by some, is the removal of those things we cherish most.

What if WE viewed loss as the opportunity to begin again,
more intelligently, would that be wise?
Let's summarize,
the decades of loss prepare us for the next hill,
the next valley and ultimately, the mountain we must climb…
Take a knee or two, for a brief, emotion filled prayer;
and begin again, more intelligently.

Enigma

I spent some time trying to understand the conflicting curiosity in my mind.

Because I was confused by the idea of being in awe, so I tried to contemplate, how I would and could truly relate,

or even appreciate natural beauty up close;

a vision of beauty unimagined, undefined, and unlimited;

NOT because of breast and butt, but a smile...

yes a smile and presence that is authentic and original.

So, I started the search for a word that would help me with my dilemma...

that word is Enigma.

Wikipedia defines enigma as a person or thing, complicated, mysterious, puzzling and difficult to understand.

Let's start here...

There is a simplicity in exchanges, when chemistry exists;

yet the complexity of ONE'S mind could cause ONE'S thoughts to drift.

There is nothing mysterious or puzzling, in the emotional shift when precious time is shared;

yet some would like to make it difficult for their own personal gain.

Can WE truly ask why ONE never sees the answers,

when they never KNOW the questions?

That's why THOSE who are an enigma, appreciate and reciprocate what is NEEDED to be understood and that's all this ONE has to say!

Trust Beyond Compare

A passionate kiss was the end result of the moments
which led to this;
Let's take a few steps back
to the initial discussion and conversation...
Do you want to know me, or do you want to KNOW me?
I tried to find the words that would satisfy the justice
this unique person has shared,
and who has gained my respect
by their actions and their presence.

They quietly reciprocate respect by sharing
THE most precious resource to us all...
TIME.
Blind trust is the ability to not see those things in front of you,
and still move about the world.
Trust, but Verify— requires that we ask an additional source
to confirm what we THINK we know.
Trust beyond compare demands that we BELIEVE
what we are, what we perceive, and what we feel.
With your actions, I KNOW you want to KNOW me,
I believe you respect me, and I BELIEVE you shared something
more precious than time...
you shared your space.
For that I am grateful, as your actions truly are—
Trust Beyond Compare.

Attention

Your presence demands attention.

Your character requires respect.

Your conversation- once understood- ensures the question, 'now what?' after great sex.

Most average men miss these points, but I don't; because, as U KNOW, I am not average.

Intent

        MY intent is to respectfully enjoy you,
        and all that you have to offer.
        If it is just a smile and a kind word or gesture,
        that's fine.

Intent has nothing to do with expectations—
as I have none—
yet what I am willing to appreciate
and accept have no limits.

        Be open and honest with yourself
        and all that is natural, will be shared.
        Your personal constitution must guide
        your actions and decisions.

YOUR intent, spoken or otherwise,
will only be revealed when given the opportunity to do so...
don't take advantage of patience and kindness
that are a part of my character;
but utilize them to enable mutual benefits...
        if that is YOUR intent.

A Whisper... Don't You Know?

What makes us smile?

                Comedy, resulting in laughter.

            Good lovin, before, during and after.

       Pure silence conceived in deep thought.

       Pure joy of a gift, shared, but not bought.

              Unmitigated euphoria and utopian glow?

                  To live, love, and grow...

Imagine the view from the peak at its highest point.

Puff, puff, pass the virtual joint—

that frees and liberates our mind,

which cradles our heart and protects our soul.

    Stay focused and level, because no gain is too great,

           no loss too low;

        as cells regenerate,

    we must continue to grow...

        simply from a whisper,

                      or don't you know?

The Smile I Asked For...

I asked for a smile, and I received a sunrise.
To my surprise,
> you sat down,
>> and time paused;

You listened to an old man re-live his youth,
As he told stories of the truth,
you smiled again and for that I thank you!
But, will the exchanges and conversations and opportunities to
> know more...
>> and then I pause.

> Rest assured, when you smile at me, I smile back;
>> not because it is what you expect.
>>> It is out of respect,
> for what I see, what I might desire and for what I might share.
>> Are you curious?

Innocence Behind A Smile

We know there are 5280 feet in a mile;
We believe that trust in agape love last a lifetime.
Yet, why do we struggle with how long is a while?

Let's start here...

Can we trust the innocence behind a smile?
The smile draws us in,
or even a simple grin,
gives us warmth like the sun.

That special smile,

which has us closer to the windows to one's soul...

your eyes;

Oh yes, your eyes give us comfort
when all is lost and life is rough;
It is tough enough to not stare at the frame,
which puts the "average" woman to shame!

And yet it all started with an innocent smile?
A while is long enough to gaze into those eyes,
stare at the natural beauty and enjoy these just the same...
as long as the innocent smile, ensures mutual joy...

For a long, long while!

The Joy In The Smile That I Gave You

A smile is super-imposed on a face;

    a human canvas,

        that cannot be erased.

(pause   for   Joy   #1).

Joy #2:

    The eruption of those internal enzymes in your body,
        that invoke THIS JOY,

            transmitted thru the air...

Take   me   THERE.

A euphoric state—
where I contemplate
a reciprocal action,
to confirm THE JOY
I receive from your smile.

        If you want THAT JOY,
        walk a virtual mile with me,
        and we will see OUR JOY

thru   your   smile...

    Because I gave it to you!!

Who Is Concerned About My Lips?

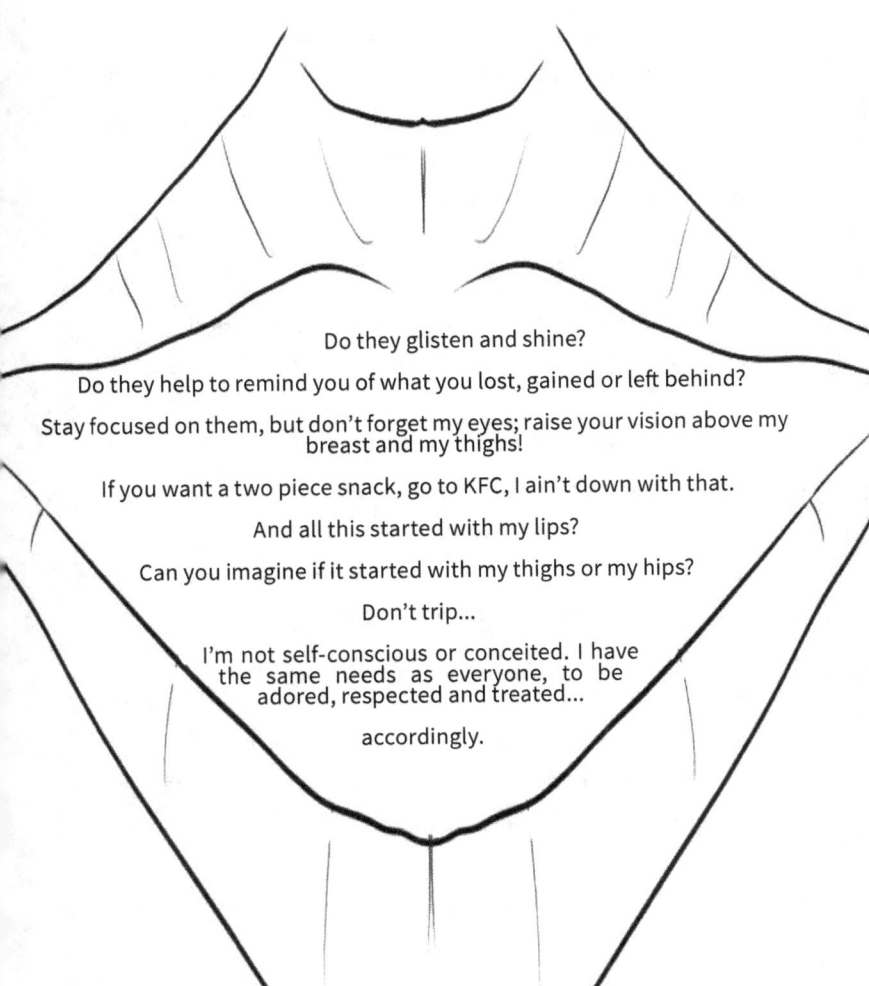

Do they glisten and shine?

Do they help to remind you of what you lost, gained or left behind?

Stay focused on them, but don't forget my eyes; raise your vision above my breast and my thighs!

If you want a two piece snack, go to KFC, I ain't down with that.

And all this started with my lips?

Can you imagine if it started with my thighs or my hips?

Don't trip…

I'm not self-conscious or conceited. I have the same needs as everyone, to be adored, respected and treated…

accordingly.

What Do I Have to Apologize For?

There is no apology needed for the love I have
I will and I plan to give you...

There is no 'I'm Sorry' in any action I have
or will take as YOUR woman...

Hopefully your wife.

Life as I have lived it, is to HONOR you
as the man who had my heart.
Do I deserve to be blocked,

left *alone*,

to beg for what others naturally receive?

F*** No;

grow up!

Respect is bidirectional—

received and given to those who earn the right,

the privilege and have the insight,

to know and believe, in your soul,

that from MY soul, I LOVE YOU....

Can you say the same?

If   not,   cut   me   loose,

let me go and be with those who will
EVENTUALLY take advantage of what I plan to nurture,

extend and grow!

I have nothing to apologize for, but you do—

and when you do,

you can have ALL OF ME BACK!!

Unappreciated Beauty

One could argue that a blind man
can hear music that moves him;
yet the unseen beauty he misses,
can only be described by another.
Just as a deaf man cannot hear
the beautiful music or sounds of nature,
that make us smile during a long life.

Still this poet,
    has not addressed the
        unappreciated

b   e   a   u   t   y   .

    It's simple:
        The lazy man can see the external attributes
            that cause the obvious reaction;
        the educated man can read or write about
            what they believe beauty is;

But the man who has LOVED and LOSS,
is the only one who can articulate the unappreciated beauty.

    To be sexy and attractive fuels the desire
    to see the unappreciated beauty YOU HAVE!

I Do See...

There is a beauty that is hidden by society's desire
to look for the norm.
There is a reality that this beauty unappreciated,
cannot and will not be respected.

> So, I ask, why you hide from someone worthy
> of the opportunity to see and enjoy the beauty
> the average man cannot and will not see?

Those who look upon you in drunken awe,
could and will never see you in suspended bliss.
Don't waste what I DO SEE!

Bees

Bees are to honey,
as mollusks are to the pearl;
Never look past the sweetness or taste
given by the natural joy granted without knowing why.

A pearl is cultivated by the agitation and friction,
yet the notion that bees make honey because they can?
So, if they can,
    you can
        and we can...
            because it *beez* that way sometimes!

Want and Won't

> What I want, versus what I won't do,
> are two different things.

What I fear is not stepping "out there"
at the same time you do...
For what I want to know is
that *you* won't leave *me*.

> So, I want you.
> I want to 'need' you,
> and I want to look at no one else
> but *you*.

But, I won't accept being less than the 'only one.'
I won't be hurt ever again,
and I won't accept lies from EITHER of US!

> What do you want,
> and what won't you do,
> to have 'me only and always'?

Poetic Words

Poetic words express the thought,
before and after "that" feeling.
They can be the difference for the sad or the sick,
moving them to the eventual healing.
Independent of the sense of circumstance,
that forces the pause before the cause;
the words before the *ooooo*,
and the words that get you thru!

>This poet can move you both
>to the place where you are from,
>OR to the place from which
>you would prefer to come.

Regardless, poetic words are the written
                           and *enunciated* words of passion!

Me, We, Us

Me, is real short of us...
yet the we, one might seek, misses the mark.
Can you hear the silence that sound has offered?

        Like paint to a canvas, the us, could be a work of art.
      Like vision without seeing; and sight without being, desire
             without knowing and lust without meaning.
      Not knowing why we look, dare I say stare, without feeling?

Because the WE is greater than you;
and the us is less than the we....feel me!

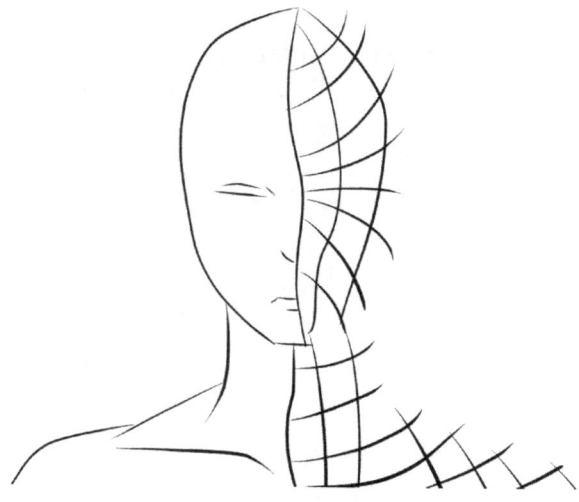

You & Me, Became Us

Emotion moves some to lose control of their faculties.
To me, as it relates to losing one's way,
it is easy to say,

> "It's not *me*,
>
> but *U*."

A genuine smile will cause, *U* not *me*, to pause;
yet U, as a reflection of WE,
will appreciate the energy not wasted on a frown.

Can we agree that the world is much better
because the combination of you and me, became *US*?

Mirror 4 U or Us

The internal mirror reflects only the smaller image of U!

There was a time, that I could not see
        beyond U
                to US;
yet when the mirror broke,
the pieces all landed in my hands.

C   u   t   s   ,

S   l   i   c   e   s   ,

B   r   u   i   s   e   s   ,

            still pieces of
j   o   y   .

                Feelings, soul exposed,
                    but *what for*?

        4 U or for US?

Your Birthday

The euphoria of birth is extended on one's birthday,
The pleasure and presence of friends
ensures the sustained enjoyment.

>Yet, the notion of Agape Love,
of those who salute you,
is what it is really all about.

Happy Birthday, long life,
and embrace those who simply
enjoy the idea of who you really are!

Much Love!

Courage

If I had courage,
here is what I might say:

> Give us one, two, or even three days
> uninterrupted, to enable the joy
> your presence always conveys.

> Pleasure is a given;
> Euphoria is the goal.
> Please do this before
> my interest grows old!

Well, if I had the courage,
all things would flow.
Because my word is better than a promise
and this, you already know!

Being In Love...

Being in love is not knowing,
yet owning up to be being;
while someone else says,

> 'YOU are doing things
> YOU said YOU never would'.

Ignore those who challenge the glow;
acknowledge those who have seen you
and know that you are...

> Cherish the one who made you so.

Because true love is raging,
Agape love is eternal,
and superficial love is fleeting.

> WALLOW in the moment,
> the notion, and the concept,
> of BEING IN LOVE.

Ambition

Ambition is the mixture of
    desire,
        persistence,
            & patience.
It is a subset of passion—
guided by satisfaction,
supported by metaphysical bliss...
Where a virtual kiss becomes real;
an idealistic thought becomes an action...

    Where eventually, ambition with enough motivation,
        enables simplistic, mutual utopian joy!

To Be Honest

To be honest, benefits can be interpreted in many ways;
Holistically, they should be mutual...
Generally, benefits should add value,
 yet value must be consumed individually.

                                                  Let's dig deeper...

Values are two-fold:
> Tangible — what we receive and touch;
> and intangible — what we feel and can't see.
> I offer and will receive both.

To offend is not part of my character;
the benefits and value that make me who I am —
that drive my actions and decisions —
should never be considered disrespectful as we discussed.

> To be honest, the chain of events that encompass
> > or make up how we perceive things;
> and become who we are AND govern how we respond
> > to how we are approached and engaged.
>
> To be honest, I would offer that you are cursed with beauty,
> intelligence, and a sexual presence.
> Shame on those who can't appreciate these qualities
> without offending.
> I know I have appreciated them and will continue to do so...
> unless told otherwise.

Can't... Now What?

Can't find the bread crumbs you once dropped.
Can't use the compass that always guided my thoughts.
Can't see my way based on the fog that mis-direction brought.
Can't find the paper for the pen your inspiration once wrought.

The true artist conveys paint to canvas and music to the sheet;
challenging the internal demons they fought.
Yet, thru all this, there was an intense
moment of lust, passion, and intimacy
we both wanted, had, and sought.

NOW WHAT?

What conversation do we seek beyond THAT moment?
What will the NEXT moment bring
that character & presence, never had bought?
What made Guinevere choose Lancelot?

Simply put...

NOW WHAT?

Moved – Inside Out?

What she feels is different from what she senses;
What she needs is
much more important than what she wants.
>What she desires at 20,
>>is much more intense @ 40;
>>>The motherhood she earned at 38,
>>>>enables the blessing
>>>>of being a grandmother at 60.

To have been moved from the outside in
is episodic, periodic, and temporary.
To have been moved from the inside out,
leaves no doubt about
the steps, the path, and the cycle.
She can only be truly moved and come full circle,
>>when moved from the inside out.

Missed Connections

Imagine not having an imagination,
or being stripped of all creative thought.

>Imagine having a planned path,
>that you KNOW GOD placed you on,
>then somehow you got lost.

Imagine, if you can, the struggle between
what FEELS right and what IS right.
Picture, if you can, the missed train,

>the delayed plane,
>that enabled THE CONVERSATION of your life...

>Are you willing to wait at that 'intersection'?

Some say a mind is a terrible thing to waste;
yet, a soul is an unimaginable thing to lose...

>Can you see the connection?
>Misdirection,

not enough time spent and lost opportunities will cause the
lack of faith that leads to loss of sight.

Seize the moments, Embrace the affection and you just might
make up for the all those Missed Connections.

Future, My Happiness & Acceptance

There is a future, short of the present,
does not guarantee your happiness.
Pause for a moment to be unhappy
with the thoughts LOST in a series of moments—

>Lost in the present...

>>Lost in past neglect.

Let's resurrect the notion that when we LOSE
we have not lost the ability to be more than we are,
nor even less than we have ever been.
Yet acceptance IS NOT accepting
what does or does not work...

>My happiness is sustained
>with the belief that FUTURE acceptance,
>allows me to wait for your joyful noise...

>When I move YOU!

A Final Chat

A final chat is always useful,
if we do what one's heart compels us to.
"We are the decisions that we make," is a phrase,
that enables the actions inside the maze of many turns.
The idea that burns and yearns for the soul to be mute
to the thoughts our hearts wish to silence.

Grasp this notion:

> The negative thoughts our intellect can cause us to
> admonish, could lead us to
> the 'decisions we don't make' tragic at best.

> So don't rest on these thoughts.

Thought

The unspoken word between rivals—
    almost enemies—
who once respected each other;
the conversation never had,
because the idea of a good conversation

cost   too   much.

The question without an answer,
or to be lost without thought,
never escapes the nimble mind.
Common sense is no longer common anymore.

Why Ask *Why*?

        The art of thought is lost on those
    who no longer think beyond what is given to them.

Awareness

Can't be searched for—
    it is subliminal,
        it is innate,
           it stays with you
when all other senses yield to misguided fate.

    Awareness drives the criminal
    to search for a new profession
    based on the lessons of multiple incarcerations
        endured to date.

Lack of awareness is a compass without a needle,
Google without a search outcome,
and faith without a higher power.

        Stop.

        Higher Power?

    Allah, Buddha or Jesus—
    find one, follow one, and believe in something;
    AND only then will true awareness be with you,
    and will never forsake you.

Loyalty?

Is only relevant in the context of
AND satisfied with current circumstances;
yet, integrity without loyalty has no sense of presence
beyond knowing why joy cannot be sustained
without internal peace.

Be grateful for those who grant you
        serenity without a cost,
                harmony without music,
                      and silence inside sound.

    As such loyalty is always around when it is earned!

A Greater Loyalty

A child's loyalty is created at the moment of conception—

It is nurtured during gestation,

first revealed at birth,

and consummated with its first breath

and latching on of the breast...

It is confirmed by the peaceful nap

it takes on it's mothers chest.

This unspoiled loyalty grows in the agape love

it receives and the path God places it on.

An adult's loyalty is the collection of affections

thru life experiences on this path;

The events that challenge the faith

and belief that our personal constitution

guides our decisions and steps.

Be ever aware that loyalty may waiver

based on the fragility of human nature;

Our actions that yield negative and positive song.

Specifically, a man's loyalty can be measured

by the sincerity deep in his gaze, the sensuality of his voice,

and the generosity of his touch.

There is no limit to the depth of his being

when loyalty is given freely and

without the expectation of reciprocation.

Such a notion is embraced by those

aware of the void lack of loyalty introduces.

Can you see, feel, and wallow in my loyalty?

Sense It, Feel It, Trust It

Short of sight, there is a sense...
a constant rhythm that we dance and smile to.

Can you imagine trusting the unknown
over & for something we desire —
unseen.
        Yet, we feel it is the right thing to do?

                Sense it, Feel it...
                    Trust it!

Consistency

> Some people laugh at consistency
> because they can't do it;
> They can't find the pleasure in being a
> reliable, available, and financial fit.

What makes the discussion about
hunters and farmers take precedent?
Is the real debate about 'field or house niggers?'
Well are these appropriate for the time frame we are in?

The oppression we suffered
once upon a time was direct;
where today it is indirect and financial.
We can no longer wait for society
to help us find our way.
Simply put, be the hybrid that is
economically fit, socially aware, and historically educated.

Disagree violently, and consistency will be fully appreciated.

Infinity

From Alpha to Omega;
Some look for the end,
before the beginning.
Yet history shows us that
the earth never stops spinning,
and life's lessons continue to start

again   and   again.

Never look past the quiet, reserved person,
as their character will have something to share...
Could be a moment in time,
a simple glance, or stare.

Yet, be cautious of the loud and outspoken,
as they drain the very sense of our existence;
and our resistance makes us question,
"Is the attraction really there....
from that moment to Infinity?"

Testing The Principle of Discretion

Discretion is a lesson
I learned at an early age;
and as I grow older,
I have become a sage of the art.

> What concepts make up the principle?
> What is discretion?
> Why ask these questions
> of someone who knows?

Enough questions on the subject,
as it causes lack of discretion from the start.
Innate trust, belief in things unseen;
moving beyond the unknown,
while being aware is what's known
in the world you own.

> Accept that these words
> are being shared because
> the concept is well within your reach;
> unless the concept escapes us both,
> and our world of belief is blown.

Is discretion a part of your personal constitution,
and fused to your core?

Nothing

With broken pen and bruised heart,
I can write nothing.

The void that fills the emptiness
that yields the b***s*** that flows from scarred,
ruined and damaged spirits...
Damn, that's harsh.

Let's applaud those that DON'T realize this about themselves:

Disheveled, with no path forward or back,
no direction or sense of purpose;
Just existing on the fragile egos OR with some,
the lack of self-confidence their souls emit.

Wow, what a way to act AND so cruel is the ABSOLUTE TRUTH...
When I have said NOTHING.

Look Up

How can we challenge YOU to be more?
With the weight of the unknowing carried,
is a burden often ignored.

>Can YOU imagine the desire (pain)
>of those who LOOK UP to you;
>as you look up to those
>who don't deserve your escalated praise?

Raise the elevation of your expectations.
Raise the manner in which you are perceived,
and thus, how you are known.

>Give ALL to those that interact with YOU—
>that this notion that you have
>the worldly confidence of just being YOU...
>Enough said, just LOOK UP!

Presence

Suspended time is trusted to no one.
The notion that some could
look beyond the current moment,
expecting tomorrow to be better than NOW...

                                                            Bores some.

Boredom infects those with
        no enjoyment of past,
                nor a vision of the future.
They lack the PRESENCE to accept the PRESENTS
granted them in both time elements.

Try this:
        Today is yesterday's tomorrow,
      AND this is a moment I am glad I did not miss!

Searching

Searching for words—
>a phrase;
Searching for a thought,
>undeserved praise.
Searching for the better me,
Searching for the unique you?

>Google, Bing, and Yahoo don't have it.
>Facebook, FaceTime, and Instagram can't capture this.
>Searching for sustained and external bliss.

Hope?

To get from there to here,
To travel with joy and have no fear;
To believe that all statements made
in your direction are sincere,
To know how Lancelot secured Guinevere...

You must have hope!

HOWEVER, Hope is not an execution strategy.
As in all things, put in the work to make it so.

Insecurity and Beauty

Insecurity and Beauty
are the rare combination
that encourages self-pity,
enables misunderstood audacity,
and extends fear, uncertainty, and doubt (FUD).

Too often, uncertainty comes
from the unwanted, cold stare,
that never warms your soul;
leaving you to ask yourself,

what the f*** was that all about?

Don't let the actions of negative people
knock you off the top shelf;
because you were placed there for A reason.

I will give you three.

You faced me, you trusted,
& will continue to trust me;
and I believe you will keep your word.

Being beautiful & sexy are extra...

like icing & ice cream.

Don't let being selflessly humble
become ammunition for those
who look up to admire—
where you alone, belong—
because they know they cannot stand there;
and if they tried, it would be absolutely wrong!

Insecurity is nurtured
by your subconscious awareness
that those around you
seek their own limelight,
before acknowledging yours.
As these same people
linger on the edge of your glow...

                        Just so, they might be noticed.

Could fear, uncertainty, or even insecurity
be that low moan deep inside you
that yearns for the simple confirmation
                that YOU ARE beautiful,
and need not ever be insecure!

Accept this confirmation in the form of a question:
                Do you remember the six words?

I'm In A Dark Room

I'm in a dark room,

                                                but I can still see.

I don't move,

                      but can hear my heartbeat.

    And I can hear familiar cries, and I can see familiar eyes
        But behind those familiar cries and familiar eyes,
            are unfamiliar demons ready to rise.
        I close my eyes and quietly shake my head.
          I want to wake up so bad,
            but those familiar cries pull me back instead.
I could leave this hollow room— to you and to them,
     but the cries...
            They sound like home.
They sound desperate and they sound alone.
            They're loud and it hurts.
"I have found a way out," I say;
but the familiar eyes don't want to move.
The familiar cries are still there,
but they are happy where they are—

                                    so they have said.

I turn to leave and finally see,
to my astonishment, my own demons ready for me.
The demons are silent, and the demons move.
Within the poorly lit room,
you have been spoken for and you are no more.
I realize the cries are yours.

The demons have you and are coming for me...

By passing through you.

Integrity With Personal Amendments

Integrity ignored by some,
is respected by even less,
and is steered by the rules
that govern your life.

> Better stated, your personal constitution
> is arbitrated by the decisions you make,
> the related actions you do, and sometimes,
> more importantly those you don't take.

When we challenge our constitutional amendments,
as age and gravity skew and upset
the vision of what once was versus what now is...
We must reflect and respect that change is inevitable.

However, integrity based on protocols,
must be supported by prayer—
that protects us, fulfills us, and helps sustain us...

> Prayer is ever constant.

The Danger of Logic

Why do we accept the Truth,
when the Absolute Truth is what we truly seek?
More or less, logic contains no emotion;
and from any point of view,
there is no emotion in logic—

    and it seems that the inverse is consistently true.

Said differently, the inverse of a lie,
based on logic or emotion,
is still a non-truth.
Thus, we cross over into the danger zone
complicated with inaccurate, non-logical facts.

                                      Stop this!

That's enough of this s***!
I have lost control of the logic,
speaking emotionally of course.

Consume Ideals... Digest Reality

> I have never looked past any mutual interest,
> nor should anyone ever miss the opportunity
> for a grand entrance.

> I will not smile when I am not happy,
> and I cannot sustain a frown
> when joy cannot be found.

> So, find the focused intensity
> when you share and consume ideals
> that become part of your soul.

> Then digest reality.
> The hardest thing in life
> is the day to day!

Will, Fate & Grace

There is a sustained whisper that
all poverty stricken souls can hear;
>There is a soulful orgasm
>in the not too distant future,
>should one have the faith
>to simply draw it near.

There is a mutual will that can achieve
Grace, simply with a nod;
beyond the imperfect steps,
on the path derived from our lost thoughts.
>One can only dream and imagine
>the poverty removed from a soul
>restored thru Will, Fate, & Grace.

What's The Difference?

What's the difference between yes and maybe....

                          Maybe and no?

                        Some would say it's money.

        Let's take money off the table.

                      Where does that lead the discussion?

        It moves to a slow pace,

        as with any race,

        tempo and meter foregoes

        the desire to be rushing.

Some should say,

        "That character and temperament change

            under my dominant power.

        Lives once touched by me, become tune."

                              Yet that ain't enough.

Very talented people with influence and power,

have been looked past and thru,

just because it was not the right time.

                So what's the difference?

Physical presence, melodic sound,

and a voice that causes a silence—

that ensures time is not a criteria in the discussion.

So, every minor no, is a wanting to be a maybe;

and every maybe desires to be a yes, with time.

Translucent, Opaque, and Transparent

Remove the TRANSLUCENT film life has
placed on the lenses by which we
often view the rest of the world.

Take a moment to be impressed by those
on bent knee, not the OPAQUE nature of this world.

Be faith filled and faithful
to the TRANSPARENT prayer
created in HIS WORLD.

Thank GOD daily for grace,
and HIS vision will be fulfilled.

Are We Truly Grateful?

Most of us give thanks for the food
we are about to receive;
yet some of us can't believe
the lack of appreciation of God gifts that are so

s   i   m   p   l   e   .

> Let us take a moment to smile upon the moments,
> the people, and acts that make us grateful.

Grateful for family, friends, and the unions given.
Grateful for each day, the life, and company
in which we are allowed to live.
Grateful for the health, each breath, and step we take.
Grateful for the impression of the mere presence
of those with whom we rest and wake.
Just be grateful for goodness sake!

Breathe and Let Go

The universe in which we reside,
requires measured steps for the outcomes we seek.
Each breath we take,
each gasp our self-directed, desire filled actions,
puts us on a path walked by only a few...

        Don't pause to watch the view.
Embrace the notion that we control the passion,
that our focused efforts, resulting in outcomes
have no endless pleasure...

        So continue to seek the selfish treasure.
Accept that the opportunities of self-discovery
increases our appetite and desire to be at peace—
both mental and physical—
proportional to a self-indulged joy.

        Breathe and let go, for goodness sake!

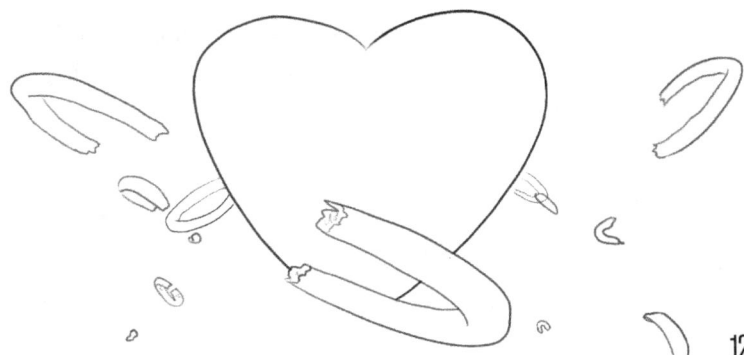

Why Are We Here?

There is an undeniable,
>   undisputed
>> truth of why we are here.

Yet, as we search for the excuses
to explain our absence and
relapses into lost time,
we realize that unfiltered joy
IS not at the top of our list.
Dare we suggest that lost time ensures
we are conscious of joy, filled with passion...
perceived, and therefore realized,
by the emotion with the notion of accountable time?
> Simply put, we lose time for the pure joy
>> that we have IT to use;
>> however, when it costs us more,
>>> why do we lose our way?
>>> Why are we here?
>>>> We are trying to recapture lost time,
>>>>> and valuable ways to fill it.

Treasure, Recognition and Purity

To escape expression unmitigated,
To have lost unremarkable thought
for the simplistic recognition,
AND the ability of creativity in every ART form,
is beyond most.
Yet, the purity of undeniable expression
never released by the original thought provoker,
is without reason.

Just as the true essence
of beauty is never captured—
it can only be the absolute treasure
just beyond the moment it was realized.
Pleasure me—

> not for the ability to smile
> when all others frown.

Forgive me—

> not when all others miss the opportunity
> to appreciate more than you will ever be,
> and less than they will ever become.

> The treasure of our recognition,
> and the purity of our thoughts,
> is all that we will have in our creative construct.

So, What Is Earthly Success?

Is it the acknowledgment of someone
who holds your thoughts in suspense?
Is it the appreciation
that your interest is reciprocated?
Is it that your attention
and affections are appreciated?

Or is merely the notion that
a few series of emotions and intimacy
can fill a lifetime of void?

Why do these keys dissolve in the hands of so many
who simply don't understand the true worth
of another's presence?
Such is the border between these keys
and being treated as a fool;
AND the focus of passion not absorbed.

Things More Important Than $...

Things more important than $!

A compliment, with respect,
that one did not expect.
A smile— that can last a life time;
while money, is a short time thing.

> Can you imagine a day with no light,
> and a night with no sleep?
> Can you see past the idea or notion
> that destiny allowed me to meet you today
> without money?

I appreciate the natural beauty
that GOD gave you,
don't change a thing.
Money can't purchase character,
it can't change the perfect view of beauty,
and it won't change how I see you!

Humble

Real or fake is not a matter of body or shape,
it's a function of facts.
How one acts and reacts in the moment,
when we are challenged to be more than we once were;
and to be more than we are—

                                                yet be humble.

For goodness sake, be humble.

Earthly to Spiritual?

A glass of water— no, ice.
Simply asked for, promptly provided.
The earth's finest natural liquid,
underestimated, underappreciated, and under protected.
Water is one of the few earthly things
that we must have to sustain us.

Can we move from the earthly to the spiritual?

The vast majority have a higher power,
that 'guide our steps and control our lives;'
yet our spirit does not always give tribute.
We refuse to take the simple steps
or acts that can sustain our soul.

Let's try this.

Give honor and praise to the owner
of our eternal spirit—
THE ONE on high.

For me, Heavenly Father,
I am grateful for each and every blessing;
Collectively, and for every individual—
I thank YOU for everyone reading these words!

Vision For A Blessing

Where does emotion take us
when we can see the outcome?
Where does logic take us
when we don't know from whence, we have come?
How do we ensure that our brief view of the present,
causes marked time to be less than we expected;
yet we are not surprised by the reflected images in our future?
How can we enjoy the instant pleasures that are granted,
yet pass on what is virtually promised?

VISION is the things seen,
yet appreciated from a distance;
but not yet fully understood, accepted, or encapsulated
in the MIND'S EYE of life fulfilled.

Look beyond what is currently
in OUR grasp, OUR reach, and OUR abilities;
and explore the ABOVE AVERAGE, with vision—
logic and emotion removed.

As such, GOD WILL BLESS YOU!

This Side of Calm

As aspiring students,
we looked for the euphoric state.
As growing adults,
we continue to seek God's Grace.
Counting from infinity back to one,
ensures the thought has just begun—
to enable the appropriate reverse
in one's own mind, guarantees
the clear view of the universe;
with deafening silence,
and the absolute confidence of innate trust,
we find ourselves with limitless boundaries.

So, let this be known:
> That from dusk til dawn,
>> from the day we were born,
>>> we have always tried to find
>>> this side of calm.

Why Can't You Stay?

Many have written about 'being down for the cause;'
then something happens that made them pause
enough to make them WANT to leave...

> Then THEY stayed!
> Let's be blunt!

You can stay on my lap,
but get out of my mind;
You can stand on my porch,
just don't show me that big behind.
If you can comprehend the distracted,
rambling words, we search for...

> Why can't YOU stay?

Let's go back...

The initial disrespect WE accepted
was because no one wants to challenge,
or remember the conversation that left the residue...
So let's let that go,
AND go further back.

His-Story dictates and demands
that WE cannot, and WE will not accept
being asked to leave the porch—
to go around back to receive
what WE naturally expect out front….

So why talk about laps and behinds,
IF these are the natural distraction
His-Story wants US to focus on?

                                         SO, why can't YOU Stay?

YOU has historically been US,
when WE can find and remain together.
AND if WE can't stay,
then all that WE have worked for
is LOST and so are WE.

                                              So, WE must stay!

Find Me...

When the world jumps up and down,
turns inside out and pauses—
not for OUR collective trials and tribulations.
I will be there...

>NOT because I HAVE TO,
>but because I CHOOSE TO CARE!

To care for those I respect and adore,
simply for the mutual appreciation
of life's most straight forward pleasures.

>FIND ME!

Heavenly Father, When I

Heavenly Father, when I
don't have the strength
to help others,
>please *help me*.

Gracious Lord, when I
lose my way,
>please *find me*.

When I am lost and distracted,
>*guide me*, Precious Savior.

Jesus, when I
do THY WILL,
>please *bless me*.

Heavenly Father, when I
know what is right and decide wrong;
when family and friends don't come first,
>please *forgive me*.

With all these things,
I will never forsake thee. AMEN.

www.ingramcontent.com/pod-product-compliance
Lightning Source LLC
Chambersburg PA
CBHW050434010526
44118CB00013B/1526